50 Extinct Dishes and How to Revive Them

By: Kelly Johnson

Table of Contents

- **Garum-Fermented Fish Sauce** (Ancient Rome)
- **Roast Peacock with Gilded Feathers** (Medieval Europe)
- **Beaver Tail Stew** (Colonial North America)
- **Salmis of Pigeon** (19th-Century France)
- **Ambergris-Infused Custard** (Renaissance Europe)
- **Turtle Soup** (Victorian England & America)
- **Stuffed Dormice** (Ancient Rome)
- **Rook Pie** (Old England)
- **Stewed Lamprey** (Medieval Europe)
- **Black Broth** (Ancient Sparta)
- **Cock Ale** (17th-Century Britain)
- **Elver (Baby Eel) Pâté** (Medieval France)
- **Mock Turtle Stew** (Victorian England)
- **Boiled Hedgehog** (Traditional Romani)
- **Wild Boar in Spiced Wine Sauce** (Ancient Rome)
- **Jellied Moose Nose** (Indigenous North America)
- **Lark Tongue Pie** (Ancient Rome)
- **Swan à la Royale** (French Court Cuisine)
- **Dodo Meat Roast** (Mauritius, 1600s)
- **Whale Blubber & Skin (Muktuk)** (Arctic Indigenous)
- **Pressed Duck (Canard à la Presse)** (19th-Century France)
- **Barbecued Passenger Pigeon** (North America, 1800s)
- **Deviled Kidneys on Toast** (Edwardian England)
- **Potted Shrimp with Bone Marrow** (18th-Century Britain)
- **Boiled Calf's Head with Brain Sauce** (Victorian England)
- **Elderflower Posset** (Medieval England)
- **Calf's Foot Jelly** (Georgian England)
- **Steamed Puffin with Crowberries** (Nordic Regions)
- **Fried Thylacine Steaks** (Tasmania, 1800s)
- **Ox Tongue in Madeira Sauce** (19th-Century France)
- **Roast Ibex with Wild Herbs** (Alpine Europe)
- **Woolly Mammoth Jerky** (Prehistoric Cooking)
- **Victorian-Style Bone Marrow Toast** (19th-Century Britain)
- **Pan-Seared Galapagos Tortoise Steak** (18th-Century Explorers)
- **Goose Blood Soup (Czernina)** (Old Poland)

- **Ragout of Dormice** (Ancient Roman Delicacy)
- **Bear Paw Stew** (Imperial China)
- **Stuffed Pufferfish (Fugu)** (Ancient Japan)
- **Braised Muskox in Juniper Sauce** (Nordic Regions)
- **Timbale of Songbirds** (French Aristocracy)
- **Savory Beaver Tail with Mustard Glaze** (Colonial North America)
- **Fried Cicada Cakes** (Ancient China)
- **Curried Woolly Rhino** (Ice Age Diet)
- **Salted Auk Breasts** (Viking Age)
- **Boiled Elephant Trunk** (Colonial Africa)
- **Stuffed Bison Hump** (Indigenous North America)
- **Nutmeg-Stuffed Oysters** (Elizabethan England)
- **Grilled Megalodon Fillet** (Prehistoric Fantasy)
- **Chilled Mammoth Fat Terrine** (Paleolithic Diet)
- **Reindeer Marrow & Cloudberry Tart** (Ancient Scandinavia)

Garum-Fermented Fish Sauce (Ancient Rome)

Ingredients:

- 2 lbs small fish (anchovies or sardines)
- 1/2 cup sea salt
- 1/4 cup dried herbs (oregano, thyme, bay leaves)

Instructions:

1. Layer fish and salt in a glass jar, pressing down each layer.
2. Add herbs and cover loosely with cheesecloth.
3. Let ferment in a warm place for 6-8 weeks, stirring weekly.
4. Strain and store the liquid in a sealed bottle. Use sparingly in dishes.

Roast Peacock with Gilded Feathers (Medieval Europe)

Ingredients:

- 1 whole turkey or goose
- 1/4 cup butter, softened
- 1 tsp saffron threads
- 1 tbsp honey
- Edible gold leaf (optional, for decoration)

Instructions:

1. Preheat oven to 375°F (190°C).
2. Rub the bird with butter, saffron, and honey.
3. Roast for 2-3 hours, basting occasionally.
4. Let rest and optionally decorate with edible gold leaf before serving.

Beaver Tail Stew (Colonial North America)

Ingredients:

- 2 lbs oxtail (or authentic beaver tail, if available)
- 1 onion, chopped
- 2 carrots, diced
- 2 potatoes, cubed
- 1 cup beef broth
- 1 tsp thyme
- Salt and pepper to taste

Instructions:

1. Sear oxtail in a pot until browned.
2. Add onions, carrots, and potatoes.
3. Pour in broth and seasonings.
4. Simmer for 2-3 hours until tender. Serve warm.

Salmis of Pigeon (19th-Century France)

Ingredients:

- 2 Cornish hens, quartered
- 2 tbsp butter
- 1 cup red wine
- 1 cup chicken stock
- 1 shallot, minced
- 1 tsp thyme

Instructions:

1. Brown hens in butter. Remove and set aside.
2. Sauté shallots, then deglaze with red wine.
3. Return hens to the pan, add stock and thyme. Simmer for 30-40 minutes.
4. Serve with sauce drizzled over.

Ambergris-Infused Custard (Renaissance Europe)

Ingredients:

- 2 cups cream
- 4 egg yolks
- 1/2 cup sugar
- 1 tsp vanilla extract
- A few drops of truffle oil

Instructions:

1. Heat cream until warm.
2. Whisk egg yolks and sugar, then slowly mix in warm cream.
3. Stir in vanilla and truffle oil.
4. Pour into ramekins and bake in a water bath at 325°F (160°C) for 30 minutes.

Turtle Soup (Victorian England & America)

Ingredients:

- 1 lb veal, diced
- 1 onion, chopped
- 1 carrot, diced
- 4 cups beef broth
- 1 tbsp Worcestershire sauce
- 1/2 tsp nutmeg

Instructions:

1. Brown veal in a pot.
2. Add onions, carrots, and broth. Simmer for 1.5 hours.
3. Stir in Worcestershire sauce and nutmeg.
4. Serve hot.

Stuffed Dormice (Ancient Rome)

Ingredients:

- 2 quail, cleaned
- 1/2 cup minced pork
- 1/4 cup chopped nuts (pine nuts or walnuts)
- 1 tsp honey
- 1/2 tsp black pepper

Instructions:

1. Mix pork, nuts, honey, and pepper.
2. Stuff into the quail cavities.
3. Roast at 375°F (190°C) for 30 minutes. Serve warm.

Rook Pie (Old England)

Ingredients:

- 4 pigeon breasts, diced
- 1 onion, chopped
- 1/2 cup mushrooms, sliced
- 1 cup beef broth
- Pie crust dough

Instructions:

1. Sauté pigeon, onions, and mushrooms.
2. Add broth and simmer until thickened.
3. Pour into a pie crust, cover, and bake at 375°F (190°C) for 40 minutes.

Stewed Lamprey (Medieval Europe)

Ingredients:

- 1 lb eel, cleaned and cut into pieces
- 1 cup red wine
- 1/2 cup fish stock
- 1 onion, chopped
- 1/2 tsp cinnamon

Instructions:

1. Sauté onion in a pot.
2. Add eel, wine, stock, and cinnamon.
3. Simmer for 40 minutes. Serve warm.

Black Broth (Ancient Sparta)

Ingredients:

- 2 cups pork broth
- 1/2 cup pig's blood (or beef blood, available in specialty markets)
- 1 clove garlic, minced
- Salt and pepper to taste

Instructions:

1. Heat broth until warm.
2. Stir in blood slowly while whisking.
3. Simmer for 10 minutes. Serve hot.

Cock Ale (17th-Century Britain)

Ingredients:

- 1 whole rooster (or chicken), cleaned and chopped
- 1 gallon dark ale
- 1 cinnamon stick
- 1/2 tsp grated nutmeg
- 1/4 cup raisins
- 1/4 cup brown sugar
- 1/2 cup brandy

Instructions:

1. Boil the rooster in water until tender, then shred the meat.
2. In a pot, mix ale, spices, raisins, and sugar. Heat gently.
3. Add shredded rooster meat and simmer for 30 minutes.
4. Strain and stir in brandy before serving warm.

Elver (Baby Eel) Pâté (Medieval France)

Ingredients:

- 1/2 lb smoked eel, chopped
- 2 tbsp butter
- 1 shallot, minced
- 1/4 cup heavy cream
- 1 tbsp lemon juice
- 1/2 tsp white pepper

Instructions:

1. Sauté shallots in butter.
2. Blend smoked eel, shallots, cream, lemon juice, and pepper until smooth.
3. Chill for 2 hours and serve with toast or crackers.

Mock Turtle Stew (Victorian England)

Ingredients:

- 1 lb veal shoulder, diced
- 4 cups beef broth
- 1 onion, chopped
- 2 carrots, diced
- 1 tbsp Worcestershire sauce
- 1 tsp nutmeg
- 2 hard-boiled eggs, chopped

Instructions:

1. Sauté veal and onions in a pot.
2. Add broth, carrots, Worcestershire sauce, and nutmeg. Simmer for 1.5 hours.
3. Stir in chopped eggs and serve.

Boiled Hedgehog (Traditional Romani Cuisine)

Ingredients:

- 1 lb pork belly
- 1 onion, chopped
- 2 bay leaves
- 1 tsp black pepper
- 4 cups water

Instructions:

1. Bring water to a boil with onion, bay leaves, and pepper.
2. Add pork belly and simmer for 2 hours until tender.
3. Serve with potatoes or bread.

Wild Boar in Spiced Wine Sauce (Ancient Rome)

Ingredients:

- 2 lbs pork shoulder, cubed
- 2 cups red wine
- 1 tbsp honey
- 1/2 tsp cinnamon
- 1/2 tsp black pepper
- 2 cloves garlic, minced

Instructions:

1. Marinate pork in wine, honey, cinnamon, and pepper overnight.
2. Brown pork in a pan, then add marinade and garlic.
3. Simmer for 2 hours until tender. Serve with bread.

Jellied Moose Nose (Indigenous North America)

Ingredients:

- 1 beef tongue
- 4 cups beef broth
- 1 onion, chopped
- 1 bay leaf
- 1 tbsp gelatin

Instructions:

1. Simmer beef tongue with broth, onion, and bay leaf for 3 hours.
2. Remove tongue, peel skin, and slice thinly.
3. Stir gelatin into broth, then pour over sliced tongue in a mold.
4. Chill until set and serve cold.

Lark Tongue Pie (Ancient Rome)

Ingredients:

- 1 lb chicken hearts, cleaned
- 1/2 cup red wine
- 1/2 tsp cinnamon
- 1/2 tsp black pepper
- Pie crust dough

Instructions:

1. Simmer hearts in wine, cinnamon, and pepper for 30 minutes.
2. Pour into a pie crust and bake at 375°F (190°C) for 40 minutes.

Swan à la Royale (French Court Cuisine)

Ingredients:

- 1 whole goose
- 1/2 cup butter
- 1 tbsp honey
- 1 tsp thyme

Instructions:

1. Rub goose with butter, honey, and thyme.
2. Roast at 375°F (190°C) for 2.5 hours, basting occasionally.

Dodo Meat Roast (Mauritius, 1600s)

(Since dodos are extinct, use turkey thigh as a substitute)

Ingredients:

- 2 turkey thighs
- 1/4 cup coconut milk
- 1 tbsp turmeric
- 1 tsp sea salt

Instructions:

1. Marinate turkey in coconut milk, turmeric, and salt for 2 hours.
2. Roast at 375°F (190°C) for 1.5 hours.

Whale Blubber & Skin (Muktuk) (Arctic Indigenous Cuisine)

Ingredients:

- 1/2 lb pork fatback, diced
- 1/4 cup soy sauce
- 1 tbsp vinegar

Instructions:

1. Dice fatback and freeze until firm.
2. Serve raw with soy sauce and vinegar.

Pressed Duck (Canard à la Presse) (19th-Century France)

Ingredients:

- 1 whole duck, roasted and carved
- 1 cup red wine
- 1/2 cup duck stock
- 2 tbsp cognac
- 2 tbsp butter
- 1 shallot, minced
- 1 tbsp blood (optional, for authenticity)

Instructions:

1. Roast the duck at 375°F (190°C) for 1 hour.
2. Carve the duck, keeping the carcass.
3. In a press (or by hand with a heavy pan), extract the juices from the carcass.
4. In a pan, sauté shallots in butter, then add wine, stock, and pressed juices.
5. Simmer until reduced, then stir in cognac and optional blood.
6. Pour over carved duck and serve.

Barbecued Passenger Pigeon (North America, 1800s)

Ingredients:

- 4 squabs, butterflied
- 1/4 cup maple syrup
- 1 tbsp black pepper
- 1 tbsp sea salt
- 1 tsp smoked paprika

Instructions:

1. Mix maple syrup, salt, pepper, and paprika.
2. Rub over squabs and marinate for 1 hour.
3. Grill over medium heat for 10 minutes per side.

Deviled Kidneys on Toast (Edwardian England)

Ingredients:

- 4 lamb kidneys, cleaned and sliced
- 2 tbsp Worcestershire sauce
- 1 tsp mustard powder
- 1 tbsp butter
- 2 slices toasted bread

Instructions:

1. Melt butter in a pan and sauté kidneys for 2 minutes.
2. Add Worcestershire sauce and mustard powder. Cook 5 more minutes.
3. Serve over toasted bread.

Potted Shrimp with Bone Marrow (18th-Century Britain)

Ingredients:

- 1/2 lb shrimp, peeled
- 2 tbsp bone marrow, melted
- 2 tbsp butter
- 1/2 tsp mace
- 1/2 tsp white pepper

Instructions:

1. Melt butter and bone marrow together.
2. Stir in shrimp and seasonings, then cook for 3 minutes.
3. Pour into a jar and refrigerate. Serve spread on toast.

Boiled Calf's Head with Brain Sauce (Victorian England)

Ingredients:

- 1 calf's head, cleaned (or 1 veal shank)
- 4 cups water
- 1 onion, chopped
- 1 bay leaf

For the sauce:

- 1 calf's brain (or 1/2 cup bone marrow)
- 2 tbsp butter
- 1 tbsp mustard
- 1 tbsp vinegar

Instructions:

1. Boil calf's head with water, onion, and bay leaf for 3 hours.
2. Mash brain with butter, mustard, and vinegar.
3. Serve sauce over sliced meat.

Elderflower Posset (Medieval England)

Ingredients:

- 2 cups heavy cream
- 1/4 cup sugar
- 1/4 cup elderflower cordial
- 1 tbsp lemon juice

Instructions:

1. Heat cream and sugar until simmering.
2. Remove from heat, stir in elderflower cordial and lemon juice.
3. Pour into cups and refrigerate until set.

Calf's Foot Jelly (Georgian England)

Ingredients:

- 1 calf's foot, cleaned
- 4 cups water
- 1 lemon, juiced
- 1/2 cup sugar

Instructions:

1. Boil calf's foot in water for 4 hours.
2. Strain and mix with lemon juice and sugar.
3. Pour into molds and refrigerate overnight.

Steamed Puffin with Crowberries (Nordic Regions)

Ingredients:

- 1 Cornish hen
- 1/2 cup crowberries (or black currants)
- 1 tbsp sea salt

Instructions:

1. Season the hen with salt and steam for 1 hour.
2. Serve with crowberries.

Fried Thylacine Steaks (Tasmania, 1800s)

Ingredients:

- 2 kangaroo steaks
- 2 tbsp olive oil
- 1 tsp black pepper

Instructions:

1. Heat oil in a pan.
2. Sear steaks for 3 minutes per side.

Ox Tongue in Madeira Sauce (19th-Century France)

Ingredients:

- 1 ox tongue
- 4 cups beef broth
- 1 cup Madeira wine
- 1 onion, chopped

Instructions:

1. Simmer tongue in broth for 3 hours.
2. Peel and slice.
3. Simmer Madeira wine and onion until reduced, then pour over tongue.

Roast Ibex with Wild Herbs (Alpine Europe)

Ingredients:

- 1 whole goat leg
- 2 tbsp olive oil
- 1 tbsp rosemary
- 1 tbsp thyme
- 1 tbsp juniper berries, crushed
- 2 cloves garlic, minced
- 1 tsp sea salt

Instructions:

1. Preheat oven to 375°F (190°C).
2. Rub goat leg with olive oil, herbs, garlic, and salt.
3. Roast for 2 hours, basting occasionally.
4. Serve with roasted root vegetables.

Woolly Mammoth Jerky (Prehistoric Cooking)

Ingredients:

- 1 lb bison meat, thinly sliced
- 1/4 cup honey
- 1/4 cup salt
- 1 tsp black pepper
- 1 tsp smoked paprika

Instructions:

1. Mix honey, salt, and spices.
2. Rub over bison slices and let marinate overnight.
3. Dry in an oven at 160°F (70°C) for 6 hours.

Victorian-Style Bone Marrow Toast (19th-Century Britain)

Ingredients:

- 2 marrow bones
- 1 tsp sea salt
- 1 tsp black pepper
- 2 slices rustic bread

Instructions:

1. Roast marrow bones at 400°F (200°C) for 20 minutes.
2. Scoop marrow onto toasted bread.
3. Sprinkle with salt and pepper.

Pan-Seared Galapagos Tortoise Steak (18th-Century Explorers)

Ingredients:

- 2 sea turtle or veal steaks
- 2 tbsp butter
- 1 tbsp lemon juice
- 1 tsp sea salt

Instructions:

1. Heat butter in a pan over medium heat.
2. Sear steaks for 3 minutes per side.
3. Drizzle with lemon juice and salt.

Goose Blood Soup (Czernina) (Old Poland)

Ingredients:

- 4 cups duck or goose broth
- 1/2 cup goose blood, mixed with vinegar
- 1 carrot, chopped
- 1 onion, chopped
- 1/4 cup raisins
- 1/4 cup red wine

Instructions:

1. Simmer broth with carrot and onion for 30 minutes.
2. Stir in goose blood mixture and red wine.
3. Simmer for another 10 minutes.
4. Serve with noodles.

Ragout of Dormice (Ancient Roman Delicacy)

Ingredients:

- 4 quails, quartered
- 1/4 cup olive oil
- 1 tbsp honey
- 1 tsp black pepper
- 1/2 cup red wine

Instructions:

1. Heat olive oil in a pan.
2. Brown quail pieces for 5 minutes.
3. Add honey, black pepper, and wine.
4. Simmer for 20 minutes.

Bear Paw Stew (Imperial China)

Ingredients:

- 1 pork hock
- 4 cups beef broth
- 1/4 cup soy sauce
- 1 tbsp star anise
- 1 tsp ginger, minced

Instructions:

1. Simmer pork hock in broth for 3 hours.
2. Add soy sauce, star anise, and ginger.
3. Cook for another hour.

Stuffed Pufferfish (Fugu) (Ancient Japan)

Ingredients:

- 2 monkfish fillets
- 1/2 cup cooked rice
- 1 tbsp soy sauce
- 1 tbsp miso paste

Instructions:

1. Mix rice with soy sauce and miso.
2. Stuff into monkfish fillets.
3. Bake at 350°F (175°C) for 15 minutes.

Braised Muskox in Juniper Sauce (Nordic Regions)

Ingredients:

- 1 lb bison meat
- 1 cup beef broth
- 1/4 cup red wine
- 1 tbsp juniper berries, crushed

Instructions:

1. Brown bison meat in a pan.
2. Add broth, wine, and juniper berries.
3. Simmer for 2 hours.

Timbale of Songbirds (French Aristocracy)

Ingredients:

- 4 quails, deboned
- 1/2 cup puff pastry
- 1/4 cup foie gras
- 1/4 cup cream

Instructions:

1. Fill quail with foie gras and cream.
2. Wrap in puff pastry.
3. Bake at 375°F (190°C) for 30 minutes.

Savory Beaver Tail with Mustard Glaze (Colonial North America)

Ingredients:

- 1 beaver tail
- 1/4 cup Dijon mustard
- 1 tbsp honey
- 1 tsp black pepper

Instructions:

1. Boil beaver tail for 1 hour to remove fat.
2. Brush with mustard, honey, and black pepper.
3. Grill over medium heat for 10 minutes per side.

Fried Cicada Cakes (Ancient China)

Ingredients:

- 1 cup cleaned cicadas (or chopped shrimp)
- 1/2 cup flour
- 1/4 cup cornstarch
- 1/2 tsp five-spice powder
- 1 egg
- 1/4 cup water
- Oil for frying

Instructions:

1. Mix flour, cornstarch, and five-spice powder.
2. Whisk egg with water and mix into dry ingredients.
3. Coat cicadas in batter and fry until golden.

Curried Woolly Rhino (Ice Age Diet)

Ingredients:

- 1 lb bison or beef chunks
- 2 tbsp curry powder
- 1 onion, chopped
- 2 garlic cloves, minced
- 1 cup coconut milk
- 1/2 cup beef broth

Instructions:

1. Sauté onion and garlic in oil.
2. Add meat and brown.
3. Stir in curry powder, coconut milk, and broth.
4. Simmer for 2 hours.

Salted Auk Breasts (Viking Age)

Ingredients:

- 2 duck breasts
- 1/4 cup coarse sea salt
- 1 tsp juniper berries, crushed
- 1 tsp black pepper

Instructions:

1. Rub duck breasts with salt, juniper, and pepper.
2. Let cure for 24 hours in the fridge.
3. Rinse and dry, then pan-sear for 4 minutes per side.

Boiled Elephant Trunk (Colonial Africa)

Ingredients:

- 1 beef tongue
- 4 cups beef broth
- 1 onion, chopped
- 2 bay leaves
- 1 tsp cloves

Instructions:

1. Simmer tongue in broth with spices for 3 hours.
2. Peel off the outer skin and slice.
3. Serve with mustard sauce.

Stuffed Bison Hump (Indigenous North America)

Ingredients:

- 1 bison hump (or beef brisket)
- 1 cup wild rice
- 1/2 cup dried berries
- 1 tsp smoked salt

Instructions:

1. Slice the hump open and stuff with rice and berries.
2. Wrap in leaves or foil and slow-roast for 6 hours at 275°F (135°C).

Nutmeg-Stuffed Oysters (Elizabethan England)

Ingredients:

- 12 fresh oysters
- 1/2 tsp ground nutmeg
- 1 tbsp butter
- 1/4 cup breadcrumbs

Instructions:

1. Place oysters in shells.
2. Top with butter, nutmeg, and breadcrumbs.
3. Broil for 5 minutes.

Grilled Megalodon Fillet (Prehistoric Fantasy)

Ingredients:

- 2 shark steaks
- 2 tbsp olive oil
- 1 tsp sea salt
- 1/2 tsp smoked paprika

Instructions:

1. Brush steaks with olive oil and season.
2. Grill for 4 minutes per side.

Chilled Mammoth Fat Terrine (Paleolithic Diet)

Ingredients:

- 1 cup rendered beef tallow
- 1/2 cup wild berries
- 1 tsp honey

Instructions:

1. Melt tallow and mix in berries and honey.
2. Pour into a mold and chill.
3. Slice and serve cold.

Reindeer Marrow & Cloudberry Tart (Ancient Scandinavia)

Ingredients:

- 2 marrow bones
- 1/2 cup cloudberries (or raspberries)
- 1 pre-baked tart shell
- 1 tbsp honey

Instructions:

1. Roast marrow bones at 400°F (200°C) for 15 minutes.
2. Scoop marrow into tart shell, top with berries and honey.

www.ingramcontent.com/pod-product-compliance
Lightning Source LLC
LaVergne TN
LVHW081336060526
838201LV00055B/2688